SOUNDS OF YOURSELF

SOUNDS OF YOURSELF

Theta Burke

DELAFIELD PRESS

Ann Arbor, Michigan

ISBN: 0-916872-03-3
Library of Congress Catalog Card Number: 76-48010
Printed in the United States of America

First Edition

From your different dreams
    your many stances
you taught me much.
And in your growing
    I increased.

SOUNDS OF YOURSELF

Learnings of the Heart

Dreaming and Working

Contemplations

Learnings of the Heart

1.

One may know all parts of himself
and make the pieces of the puzzle fit
But love is that cohesive element
essential for keeping the pieces
        in place.

2.

I feel lost in a lot of different places.
But that's because the inside finding
        is still the primary focus.
As this is achieved
I will feel at home with myself
and with all else.

3.

I will learn to be me
if I am willing to express my truth
as I come upon it
though it be different
     from that of others.

And I need keep in mind
that my perception of what is truth
will expand as I grow.

4.

When I speak
let not my words be all that is heard.
Listen also to the feeling which borns them
And allow that to correct any distortion
caused by the inaccuracy
        of my speech.

5.

The Youth said to the Giver of Gifts:
Let me learn of love
      in all its ways
as I develop the wisdom to absorb and mete out.

He was almost hesitant in his request.
He had seen shadows of the pain
that was sometimes love's companion
but he had also caught glimpses
      of the depths of the joy
known to love's disciples.
He asked only that this gift
      be revealed to him
in the measure which would allow him
      always to know
even in times of despair
that no gift could be greater.

6.

Sometimes they scoff
when they hear feelings spoken
if their hearts are not yet aware
of the existence of such.

7.

If any feel lost
it is they who have not yet learned
        to give love.
They wend their way through life
as ships without a compass
always searching.
And there seems not a port
where they may unload their cargo
and know its reward.

8.

As each learns within his heart
that which pleases himself
there is less reliance on praise from others.

9.

Isolation.
A prisoner within walls that are invisible
causing me to feel so bound
that freedom seems always too distant
        and out of reach.

Perhaps when I learn to let you care
and feel the freedom to do likewise
the walls will start to disappear.

10.

She looked down
at the broken china doll—
shattered fragments
        revealing the nothingness inside.
And she wept
because she felt that same emptiness.

But when one weeps
        for what has not yet appeared,
is there not the room for its becoming?

11.

Loving ever increases
     the power and capacity of itself.

Perhaps that's the best evidence
of perpetual motion.

12.

She dutifully worked
hours beyond that which was reasonable
because long ago
she had perceived that
    this was the source
of love and approval.

And she works on
always uncertain
    that it is enough.
And she will never be able
to accurately assess
until she discovers
the real source of approval
    which resides within.

13.

Build your castles
or your cottages.
It is a matter of preference
    and not of worth
so long as that which you build
    speaks you.

14.

Old wounds are opened.
And the pain at times
        questions the process
and can only be justified
when he who accompanies you
on that reflective and difficult journey
is endowed with love to spare
which spills over
and is available to you
for use in your own healing
without obligation.

15.

The secret of a greater love
is this:
That the littler love
is freely spent.

16.

Silences
    warm and understanding
    angry
    rejecting
    hurt
    uncertain
    questioning
    approving

The perceptive heart hears what they speak.

17.

Once upon a time
thoughts and feelings
    lived in different rooms
not comfortable with each other.
You helped me learn
    I could open the doors.

18.

He did not know
that he was untrue to me
because he had not yet learned
the truth of himself.

19.

The ability to express love
precedes the capacity to forgive.
And forgiving is the balm
      which assuages guilt.

20.

The heart that blindly trusts another's
has not yet learned to rightly trust
        his own.

21.

Hell, I think,
must be the desolation
of not knowing
      love.

And Heaven could not be more
than an ever growing awareness
      of it.

22.

Somewhere long ago — so deep
she felt a pain she wouldn't keep.
She hadn't learned it was part of love
so she shut it out
        and lost the love.

23.

He walked through Fields of Feeling
as though blindfolded
unable to recognize
     the many faces of love
turned toward him
because he did not love himself.

24.

After one's eyes have been turned to the sun,
to adequately see in a lesser light
requires some time for adaptation.

The loss of a love
        is something like that.

25.

If a love
which is truly a love
goes away,
it always leaves a heart
better prepared
to receive another.

But it may take
        a little time
before it *feels* so.

26.

If one gives only as he receives,
the capacity of his reservoir
shall never increase.

27.

Tragedy.
Two hearts in silent pain
when the voice of either
could bring joy to both.

28.

If we don't believe,
it will never be.
We can only go
where our faith can see.

29.

Clay in the potter's hands
Words from a poet's soul
Tales of a great adventure
By a storyteller told
A brush and palette
By an artist held
And music that speaks
What a heart can tell

    They all say a message
    Each its own
    Of all the things
    The soul has known

And what treasure lies in each one's art
Is what's been learned by each one's heart.

Dreaming and Working

31.

What poverty of spirit there is
for him who has not a dream.

32.

Dreams
the beginning of
becoming

Growing
not forsaking dreams
trading them perhaps

Maturity
dreams and reality
merging.

33.

Hope
is the food
of dreams.

And dreams
become the foundations
of reality.

34.

A dream we must be going toward
or there is no purpose
        to what we are and feel.
Goal focused energy
pulls things into place
as a moving magnet
        attracts scattered fragments
unto itself.

A dream
enlarging and propelling the force
called Direction.

35.

That talent which resides within
treat with reverence and great respect
      as you would an honored guest.
And say not to yourself
I am only an ordinary man
      whose house should not grace such a visitor.

I say to you
Be aware of and treasure such a gift.
It was not thoughtlessly bestowed.
You need only recognize its greatness
and provide a welcome residence
with heart and hands
      to tend and nurture
so that it may grow
and become all that it was meant to express.

36.

One earned much money.
And that is good I say
if he does not allow it
to hurt him or others.

Another received a great honor.
That, too, is good
if it does not prevent the continuation
of the effort which produced the accolade.

For neither money nor honor
should be the goal.
One or both may come unbeckoned
to him whose work
is an expression of his soul.
And that is the real joy.

There are those whose work is such
who know neither wealth nor fame
who labor in the shadows
apart from the limelight.
But they know the same reward.

37.

I watched the planes take off.
The little ones didn't need nearly so much time
or distance on the runway
      as did the huge ones.

I guess dreams are like that, too.

38.

If a love you have known
or a truth you have learned
has not expanded your vision
and caused you to glimpse
        that which might become,
then despair
and say it's all for naught.
But if
        even for a fleeting moment
you have been aware of that which to you
        is happiness
then work
press on
and make the dreams become real.

39.

Dreams
not fulfilled
may shatter and embitter
Or deepen understanding
     and increase sensitivity
to others' dreams.

40.

With their dreams for me
they went rushing on ahead
leaving me behind
        and feeling alone
trying to know what dreams were my own.

41.

After a goal is reached
we recognize
        in retrospect
that events leading to such
have been in process for awhile.

Can this thought, then, not sustain us
at other times
        when we are *in* that process
and be the means to provide the faith
that the task is being accomplished?

42.

Too often, perhaps,
we see the goal as an end
        unto itself
and miss the joy of the journey.

Contemplations

43.

A man cannot plumb depths
   in another
beyond his own level.

44.

When one gives for the receiving
the giving is diminished.

A true giver
is as a sower of seeds
who does not need to wait to see
      the sproutings
or the bearing of the fruit.
He knows that each seed will yield
      in its own time
that of which it is capable.

And someone will know
      the harvest.

45.

Belief in oneself
to the extent he knows himself
is reality.

To believe in the part
beyond that knowledge
is faith.

And the acknowledgement
of that portion
perhaps is God.

46.

Seeing evidence of the durability
        of the old
when exposure to the new
has been too much in evidence
is like a trip back home
and perspective is righted.

47.

The gardener says
    too much fertilizer
    causes plants to not pause
      long enough
    in their growth
    to produce flowers.

And I observe
    that too much concern
    with the accumulation
      of material possessions
    does not allow time for the soul
    to bear its fruits.

48.

Stay in touch with the place of your beginning.
It helps keep you aware of people
         and circumstances
that had a part in your shaping
and lends greater accuracy
to your perception of yourself.

49.

Sometimes it appears
that concern with the accumulation of years
is more prevalent with those
who have sought gratification
from physical attributes
and fear their deterioration.

They are ageless
whose beauty of mind
has properly assigned priorities
so that the passing of the years
only adds facets
which contribute to the richness of the glow.

50.

Bitterness of spirit
invades the bones
    and vitals of the body.

51.

Hold lightly those tangible treasures.
To do so increases the energy
    for developing the intangible.
And therein lies that
    which ever endures.

52.

Death is a separation
and a loss of the association.
But the meaningfulness
        of a relationship is ongoing
and is never lost.
Whatever else immortality may be
that is part of it.

53.

It shall be ineffective
when an attempt is made
        to feed a hungry soul
by one who has not yet learned
that the spirit has its resources within.

We need only point one to himself.

54.

Pleasure in one's own gifts
    and awareness of their worth
leaves little room for envy
of others' treasures.

55.

I resent your feeling responsible
      for what I do
because that says to me
you feel I am
      a lesser person.

56.

A pot boils over
      if it is too full
      if the heat is too high
      or if it is covered so tightly
that there is no room for the steam to escape.

Best we attend to such facts
regarding our lives.

57.

How sad
when he who is blind
is afraid to believe
that others have eyes.

58.

Oceans
separate
continents.

Boundaries
separate
nations.

Fear
separates
men.

59.

Sometimes we unwittingly
rob those who may love us
of comfort we could give
because we are not sufficiently aware
of our worth to them.

60.

You know already
enough of what causes you unhappiness.
Think, then, on those realities
    which give you comfort
so that this awareness shall increase.

61.

Others caused the borning of your body
but only you can allow
     the borning of your spirit.
And when you act on that realization
that is Rebirth.

62.

It's sad that so many
look to others
to tell them
        what should be enjoyable
and never learn their own tastes.

63.

Of dates and facts
some think education is.
Rather, it is the manner of use
by the heart and mind
      of all knowledge.

64.

You own only that part of yourself
which you understand and accept.
And that is the only part
which you are able to truly enjoy
    or share with another.